Freed From The Brambles

By
Danny Helms

Words of Courage, Hope and Faith

Foreward by Todd Deaver

FREED FROM THE BRAMBLES

Copyright © 2009 by Danny Helms

215 W. 15th Street

Hope, Arkansas 71801

Paperback ISBN 978-0-578-03196-5

Hardback ISBN 978-0-578-03280-1

Unless otherwise noted, all scripture quotations are from the King James Version of the Bible.

Noted scriptures NASB are taken from the NEW AMERICAN STANDARD BIBLE ®, Copyright © 1960, 1962, 1963, 1971, 1972, 1973, 1975, 1977, 1995 by the Lockman Foundation. Used by permission.

A c k n o w l e d g e m e n t s

So many people have crossed my path through my difficult times. I believe God's providence in many of these times guided our paths. Though some were harsh even to the point of being cruel not following God's commands of kindness, gentleness and loving, they too were there, I believe for a purpose. Some were truly "a puller of thorns."

A special thanks is given to Larry Culbreath, Jack Gathright and Todd Deaver who always show Christ in their lives and have displayed His love, mercy and kindness to me through most difficult times, never growing weary in well doing. May the Lord bless each of you.

CONTENTS

Foreward

If anyone besides Job is qualified to write about suffering, it's my dear friend Danny Helms. He knows it inside and out. He has felt its oppressive weight for years. He has stared it in the face—day after day, night after night. Danny knows all about suffering.

But he also knows about deliverance. Even though many of the afflictions still persist, he has experienced firsthand the healing power of God's touch—and I've witnessed the incredible change with my own eyes. I knew him when he was burdened down with sorrow, but by the grace of God he's a different man. He now has a peace, a joy, a confidence about him that would amaze and inspire you if you knew his story. I can honestly say I've never seen a more radical transformation. He once was caught in the brambles, but he has been set free.

I don't say all this simply to brag on him. He'd be the first to tell you all the glory belongs to the Lord. I bring it up to emphasize that, in the pages that follow, Danny knows what he's talking about. He speaks from the heart, and he writes from the perspective of one who has experienced both misery and joy, bondage and freedom.

If you feel trapped, struggling under the weight of heavy burdens, I believe Danny's words can help you. He's been there, and he found his way out. With God's help he has learned to soar. I hope you'll listen to what he has to say.

Todd Deaver

Minister, Author

July 8, 2009

Introduction

I most certainly am not a writer or a poet. I don't have a long list of degrees or credentials. I am not a minister, a counselor, or a philosopher. I am not a good speller. I don't know the proper rhythms, timing or styles of writing poetry. I am not anyone who would have ever dreamed of writing a book of poems for the entire world to see. I am nobody of great importance in this world. That's ok.

I am a child of His. I have not by my accomplishment but by the grace of God, the joy of being a Christian, plain and simple and hopefully, humble.

I endured many trials, pains, and losses and I found that these troubles had me by the throat. When I realized where I was, they had already trapped me within a bramble bush. I didn't think I could get out of such a terrible conflict. A conflict of desiring to serve God, and the mess I had made of my life. Yet I knew where I wanted to be. I was weak. I cried. God sent friends to help pull back the thorns of life that were stuck in my flesh one by one. A wise friend, Tony Hamilton, once told me, "Danny, getting through this situation will probably not be a sprint but a marathon." Tony was right. Though I may not be trapped as I once was, still scars and wounds hurt once in a while. I believe God's providence sent me brother after brother to help me see God's mercy, grace and love.

Along the way I found something of a wonder, something in myself, a God given talent and a passion. I somehow found the desire to become "a thorn puller." How and when this happened, I don't exactly know.

I hope these simple, humble writings remove a thorn or two in your path of life.

If you happen to be one of those in a position to remove a thorn in another's life, I desire that these writings will help you understand that the brambles and thorns are real. I intend to help you have some knowledge and tools to know what to say and how to share a burden or two. My goal is that these poems will help you realize that sometimes what appears to be a weakness in a brother or sister is parallel to the wounded traveler by the road to Jericho. The thieves in this situation may be burdens, trials, or sin. You can help or you can pass by on the other side. I sincerely hope that those of you who have difficulty in reaching the spiritual and emotional needs of others come away with a renewed desire to understand God's Word in loving your brother. It is the strong that is obligated to "cross the road" to "remove a thorn" for your brother.

"And Jesus answering said, A certain man went down from Jerusalem to Jericho, and fell among thieves, which stripped him of his raiment, and wounded him, and departed, leaving him half dead.
And by chance there came down a certain priest that way: and when he saw him, he passed by on the other side.
And likewise a Levite, when he was at the place, came and looked on him, and passed by on the other side.
But a certain Samaritan, as he journeyed, came where he was: and when he saw him, he had compassion on him,
And went to him, and bound up his wounds, pouring in oil and wine, and set him on his own beast, and brought him to an inn, and took care of him.
And on the morrow when he departed, he took out two pence, and gave them to the host, and said unto him, Take care of him; and whatsoever thou spendest more, when I come again, I will repay thee."

Luke 10:30 – 35

The Trap

Freed From the Brambles -

Many times in life, we wander astray, not watching where we are going. We are determined to exist blindly in our own little world. Without heeding the warnings we find ourselves in a place we do not want to be. A place so far removed it is difficult to forge ahead. Still, somewhere in the deepest recesses of our mind, we know. We know where we should be. We know we are not there. We know where God wants us to be. We just have gone so far that when we try to remove ourselves from the condition we are in, we feel trapped. Trapped in the brambles.

Trying to get out of this thorn covered bramble bush hurts. The harder we try to move ahead, the deeper Satan's thorns dig into our flesh.

F r e e d   F r o m   T h e   B r a m b l e s
by the help of a friend.

I have my map, my compass in hand,
traveling the road to the Promised Land.
The path set before me is straight and true.
But something is ahead; it will be hard to get thru.

Stalling just a bit to see the web
of tangled vines with thorns ahead,
the path is covered with no opening in sight,
with so many obstacles, how is this right?

My destination I see just over the hill,
I must, I must get thru, and it's my greatest will.
I can't ease through the brambles, they're too tight.
Still, I can see over the briars, the glow of a light.

Determined to proceed as my flesh is cut and torn
I pull off a briar from my side as I mourn,
With a small step deeper into the brambles I go,
I must not stop, but it's so painful and it's slow.

I try harder and harder to release the throngs of pain,
for deeper and deeper they stab at my veins.
The more I fight this thorn covered byway
the more I am tempted to stop going this way.

Someone please help me, the struggle I fear
will hold me away from the home so dear.
Let me wait, just for a moment, I have to rest
as I pray for comfort from this great test.

Please, bring me some water to quench my thirst,
for I fear the next step will surely be worse.
Help build up my strength by giving me some meat
and I'll try again tomorrow this difficult feat.

Another day has come, another day gone,
I'm not free yet, but a step closer to home.
Thank-you dear brother, you helped carry my load
along this long and difficult road.

You came with a heart of care, weeping with me as well,
strength thru stories of Joseph, Job, and of Jesus you tell.
You told God I was trapped, told of my pain every bit,
and you prayed for me to get relief, as He saw fit.

When the trumpet sounds, and when I can hear it clear
my pains will have been forgotten, and He is there.
May you be rewarded and have a home next door
Because you helped me along the road....
                              to that Heavenly Shore

"In my distress I called upon the LORD, and cried to my God for help; He heard my voice out of His temple, and my cry for help before Him came into His ears."

Psalms 18:6 (NASB)

A Treasure Once Lost –

How do we lose something that has a value so great it is beyond measure? No treasure should ever be put up on a shelf, hidden behind insignificant objects, gathering dust, out of sight for years. Time has a way of covering everything and the owner forgets about the hiding place. Still, the treasure never lost its value, only the forgetful owner. If we forget God's love for us it is losing an unmeasurable treasure.

Hopefully someone will remind us to look for that treasure, or we will help someone find theirs.

"Or what woman, if she has ten silver coins and loses one coin, does not light a lamp and sweep the house and search carefully until she finds it? When she has found it, she calls together her friends and neighbors, saying, 'Rejoice with me, for I have found the coin which I had lost!' In the same way, I tell you, there is joy in the presence of the angels of God over one sinner who repents"

Luke 15: 8-10(NASB)

A Treasure Once Lost

I once had a treasure
its worth not realized,
I lost somewhere in the world,
to me its beauty had died.

And moving thru life
the treasure long gone,
though it was covered with dust,
held its power still strong.

I hadn't thought about that treasure
that once meant so much,
until my heart was aching,
then I longed for its touch.

At first I couldn't find it
it had been lost so long ago,
but someone reminded me
look deep into your soul.

At first, just a glimpse
was all that I could see,
then with its glow so strong
it's full worth came to me.

The once beloved treasure,
no longer apart,
I grasp it tightly to me
and bind it to my heart.

With hope never again
to lose such a treasure,
for God gave it to me
it's worth beyond measure.

"But if from thence thou shalt seek the LORD thy God, thou shalt find him, if thou seek him with all thy heart and with all thy soul."

Deuteronomy 4:29

My Illness -

Hardened Heart. Heart of Stone. God doesn't dwell here anymore.

The longer God is not a focus in our lives the more Satan is and we settle for it. The odd thing is that life sometimes seems so good because there is no conflict in our lives. We just submit to cutting God out therefore Satan doesn't have to bother us anymore. He already has us as one of his followers.

> *"Because sentence against an evil work is not executed speedily, therefore the heart of the sons of men is fully set in them to do evil."*
>
> *Ecclesiastes 8:11*

My Illness

I knew that I was drinking from a well
that would make me sick from the start,
but I didn't know it caused a virus
that would grow deep inside my heart.

I thought I could handle it
and it would eventually go away,
but the thing began to convince my mind
to keep the great Physician at bay.

And still I wouldn't think about
the disease that ate at my very being,
but little by little my thoughts said it was all right
to be ignoring this nagging feeling.

Days turned to weeks, months into years,
I blocked out any notion
that anything was wrong inside
while I fed the malignant commotion.

I fed it by neglecting a cure
and indulging in pleasures of this world
It let me think all was fine
so my sickness began to unfurl.

It succeeded so much in keeping me
from my dear Lord's healing water.
My body had become accustomed to
and craved the Devil's fodder.

I abandoned my brothers
and told my self all would be ok
"You can get well all by yourself,"
could hear the malicious beast say.

Then I realized that the task
would most impossible be,
because the evil that grew inside
had become an integral part of me.

Thru all my pains, my aches,
but within my heart somewhere,
hidden way deep inside, a seed
once planted was still there.

It reminded me to come back to God,
for He said He would see me thru.
By rejecting Satan, he would flee from me,
if to Him would I be true.

So, dear Lord, please hear my prayers,
please forgive me of my faults,
my weakness and my lack of keeping
all the things that I was taught.

So soon? Have you heard me,
you have already answered my plea
Satan's fled, I'm not sick anymore,
because You are here with me.

> *"For the eyes of the Lord are over the righteous, and his ears are open unto their prayers: but the face of the Lord is against them that do evil."*
>
> *1 Peter 3:12*

Oh, Brother Peter -

Peter denied his Lord, our Lord. While we read of this, our only thought is why? Why? Can you even imagine actually being with Jesus in his day to day travels? What would it have been like if our own eyes saw the blind able to see, the lame walk, the rotting leprous skin made pure and whole once again? Awesome? Marvelous? Beyond description?

If we saw these scenes in person, how in the world could our minds and our hearts have the weakness to deny Christ? Peter denied Him. We know He lives and yet we deny Him in so many ways.

"They profess to know God, but by their deeds they deny Him, being detestable and disobedient and worthless for any good deed."

Titus 1:16(NASB)

Oh Brother Peter

Brother Peter, I ask, what happened to you & I?
Why was our faith so weak, why did we deny,
while we walk along not keeping Jesus nigh?

Peter, when they took Him you didn't even stand.
I basically did the same, I fear, being a weak man
when I denied my presence in worship once again.

Finding fault or blaming others it does often seem
is my method to confuse, and has become my theme,
and fearing trials before me, I also denied His scheme.

Asking why me? Why now? when I try so….
letting my heart be full of burdens, troubles and woe
denying he will protect and guide me where I go.

Oh, brother Peter, you denied him a third time
I now feel your tears along with those of mine,
Our hearts always pain because of such a crime.

You were with Him, a friend. I know the writings of old,
how He will not forsake us, this we are told.
For as we ask, He forgives, we stay within His fold.

For He won't deny us, even once upon that day
if we keep close to Him and follow in His way,
"I have a home prepared for you" we will hear Him say.

Thelema* of Our Lord –

Why do we resist His will? Maybe it's because we take for granted God's love. Maybe it's because we don't truly trust in Him. Maybe it's not enough faith in His promises. Maybe it's stubbornness.

His will? His will is that we all should come to know him and put Him fully in our hearts, minds and soul. But God in His wisdom and power gave us the ability to refuse. Think about this, we have the ability to refuse the almighty power of God Himself.

> *"I beseech you therefore, brethren, by the mercies of God, to present your bodies a living sacrifice, holy, acceptable to God, which is your spiritual service.*
>
> *And be not fashioned according to this world: but be ye transformed by the renewing of your mind, that ye may prove what is the good and acceptable and perfect will of God."*
>
> *Romans 12:1-2*

*Thelema (thel'-ay-mah) Greek: - desire, pleasure, will.

Thelema of Our Lord
(thel'-ay-mah)

Why does He "Will" that our
lives and hearts be true.
And why does He wish
us all happiness in this world too?

With our freedom to choose
all His desires and tasks,
we often pull far away
by not doing what He asks.

Yet we are still in His wishes,
"His Will" to be with Him,
though we are slack so often
letting our light be dim.

We are but a moment in time
just a twinkling of His eye,
still the fact He loved us so
that He sent His son to die.

To enter the kingdom we must
obey the words spoken by the "One",
so let us return His love and do the words
our Father "Thy will be done."

Healing the Wounds

Patience –

We have a choice, a very difficult choice. We can choose to continue living in the brambles where pain is constant, time is slow, death often prayed for. Or we can choose to realize that we cannot go on living a life guided by our own design. For after all, we haven't done a very good job up to this point. We can choose to be absolutely, fully committed in trusting that God CAN and WILL direct our life. If we allow Him to be our guide, our rock, our fortress we can find a way out of the brambles. His Word does have power.

Beware, it's not easy. Satan will try every lie, every temptation, and every trick he has to let you know you can't get away from him. For just one small moment in time, for one moment today …. Don't let him win. Tomorrow do it once more.

> *"For whatsoever things were written aforetime were written for our learning, that through patience and through comfort of the scriptures we might have hope."*
>
> *Romans 15:4*

P a t i e n c e

When at night upon my knees,
I ask the Lord for patience, please.

Patience of Him when my pride He sees,
when I know I'm not as humble as I ought to be.

Patience that I'll be stronger in faith the longer I live,
more patience in others, more patience to forgive.

Patience in and loving those who let me down,
for I often think perfection should in them be found.

Patience in me guiding and directing my family,
not provoking but teaching with all sincerity.

Patience for strength in keeping Him near,
both in times of happiness and in times of fear.

Patience, not anxious, knowing He holds my hand,
knowing tomorrow is only for Him to understand.

Patience in waiting the glorious appearing of God,
and the time to take me home where the angels trod.

Call On Me –

Don't ever, ever, ever, did I say "don't ever"? Don't ever forget one most important thing….. Pray.

There is nothing more to say that would be of any more value.

> *"Keep watching and praying that you may not enter into temptation, the spirit is willing, but the flesh is weak."*
>
> *Matthew 26:41(NASB)*

Call On Me

When you are troubled and are sad,
call on me and I'll listen to you.
If your burden is too great and things are bad,
call on me and I'll see you through.

When you heart needs some peace,
call on me, I know just what to say.
If you have pain and need release,
call on me, call on me today.

If you feel blue and all alone,
call on me and I'll hold your hand.
If you need someone to lean upon
call on me, I'll understand.

If you have lost your courage for tomorrow,
call on me and I'll give you hope.
If a loved one is gone and you're deep in sorrow,
call on me, I'll help you cope.

If you are lost in this world of sin and woe,
call on me and I'll show you the way.
If you seek to overcome an evil foe,
call on me, I'll make sure he doesn't stay.

I'm as close as your heart, call and you will see,
I am with you no matter what hour you call
never apart if you don't want me to be.
I am your God, comforter, protector, and giver of all.

Call on Me.

*"And I say unto you, Ask, and it shall be given you; seek, and ye
shall find; knock, and it shall be opened unto you."*
Luke 11:9

Saying Thank-You, Lord –

Man has the intelligence to analyze with microscopic detail the elements of an acorn. However, man cannot take those elements individually and put them together to create an acorn that will grow an oak. Enough said.

ALL things good come from God. Through trials and pain we must still find the good, find the reason we're here. It is only by His grace and mercy that we have His promise of eternal life through His son, Jesus Christ. How can we not be thankful? How can we not give back to the very Almighty without whom we wouldn't exist? We can't even attempt to give what God gave. We must try to give what we can.

> *"O give thanks unto the LORD; call upon his name: make known his deeds among the people. Sing unto him, sing psalms unto him: talk ye of all his wondrous works. Glory ye in his holy name: let the heart of them rejoice that seek the LORD.*
> *Seek the LORD, and his strength: seek his face evermore. Remember his marvelous works that he hath done; his wonders, and the judgments of his mouth;"*

> *Psalms 105:1-5*

Saying Thank-You, Lord

You saw me lost, in sorrow and pain,
you sent Your Son to save my soul.
You put a joy deep within my heart
and took me and made me whole.

A word of thanks sure isn't enough,
but I'll tell You what I can do.
I will tell all I see, about Your deeds,
about Your Son and You.

Often, I'll get down upon my knees
and I'll try to be humble as I can be.
I'll ask forgiveness for my trespasses that day
and acknowledge You, for blessings received.

I'll stand and sing songs of praise,
ones that honor, remembering Your holiness.
I'll sing to You while teaching others
about Your love and tenderness.

As Your Word is read, my heart I'll open wide
and let Your story dwell deep within.
I won't be ashamed of the tear on my cheek
when the story of Christ is told again.

Thinking about His broken body nailed there
when the bread is passed my way,
and I'll almost see His blood flow
with the cup I take on the Lord's day.

My sacrifice I bring isn't near as great,
for mine it's so much a minor thing to do.
Letting my lips and mouth be fruitful,
loving my brother, being good and true.

So I know "thanks" isn't enough my Lord
for I don't have a gift near of equality,
let my praise be acceptable in Your sight
because the "thanks" I give….. is "me."

"By him therefore let us offer the sacrifice of praise to God continually, that is, the fruit of our lips giving thanks to his name.
But to do good and to communicate forget not; for with such sacrifices God is well pleased."

Hebrews 13:15

Wings As Eagles –

Eagles are majestic, one of God's most beautiful creatures. Eagles about midlife must retreat to safe haven to renew themselves. They literally claw at their heads and feathers until they bleed, removing all the old and broken feathers. Then they will lie quietly in the warming sun while new feathers are grown and replaced to give them the strength and power they once knew, once again. If they don't do this they will die.

As a storm approaches often the eagle will soar above the storm to avoid its dangers. We also can soar above problems and renew ourselves with God's help.

God tells us only with Him can we "mount up with wings of eagles."

"Do you not know? Have you not heard? The Everlasting God, the LORD, THE Creator of the ends of the earth does not become weary or tired. His understanding is inscrutable. He gives strength to the weary, and to him who lacks might He increases power. Though youths grow weary and tired, and vigorous young men stumble badly, yet those who wait for the LORD will gain new strength; They will mount up with wings like eagles, they will run and not get tired, they will walk and not become weary."

Isaiah 40:28-31(NASB)

Wings as Eagles

While in the cleft of the rock we stand,
removing feathers all broken and torn,
a cleansing of this earth-tied man
of things unholy, things tired and worn.

As we view the storm before us
patiently waiting as it draws near,
anticipating the mighty cloud's rush,
embracing the wind with no fear.

With nature's surge urging us on,
taking a deep breath as time is nigh,
not letting this precious moment be gone,
praising Him with hands raised high.

Of our joy and peace we loudly sing,
high above the torrents roar,
we mount up with eagles wings
and upward toward Heaven we soar,
and upward toward Heaven we soar.

So Close, Yet So Far –

We have a saying that "being close, only counts in a game of horseshoes." Well that's the way it is with God. Being almost a Christian doesn't count. Being almost righteous doesn't produce fruit. Being close to the finish line doesn't get you a reward. Being close to what is right, is still wrong.

"King Agrippa, believest thou the prophets? I know that thou believest.
*Then Agrippa said unto Paul, **almost** thou persuadest me to be a Christian."*

Acts 26:27

So Close, Yet So Far

On that Hill of Calvary,
were many of Jesus' foes,
shouting and jeers too were heard
from the lips of those.
Laughing and mocking,
as His cross was so violently raised,
they were so close to Jesus,
but yet so far away.

Blood from our Lord's
own hands flowed, staining the ground
with each clank of the nails
as His hands were cruelly bound.
And placed upon His head
a crown of thorns braided on the way,
one touched the brow of Jesus,
but yet so far away.

Soldiers low upon their knees,
kneeled below His feet,
yet they were not there to praise,
nor were they there to weep.
But parting his garment
and casting lots was the deciding way,
four soldiers were so close to Jesus,
but yet so far away.

Being raised in the middle
of two condemned men,
but He had not one transgression
not one single sin.
One thief was forgiven,
the other was in sin to stay,
he died on a cross so close to Jesus,
but yet so far away.

Heard was "Father forgive them,"
dying for you and me,
words spoken by our Lord
while hanging on that tree.
Earthquakes and the hiding
of the sun's own shining ray,
Oh! so many were close to Jesus,
but yet so far away.

Hearing all the sacrifice
will bring a tear to our eye,
but still "a more convenient time"
is often what we sigh.
Still as His scarred hand
is reaching out for us today,
are we too so close to Jesus
but yet so far away?

If I Could Have Been There -

Sometimes when we fall, all broken, tired and weary we will tell ourselves that "only if" scenario. "Only if" I had more chances in life. "Only if" I had a better home life as a child. "Only if" I had a better education. "Only if" ...... (a million other reasons). If the circumstances in our lives would have been better, maybe they wouldn't have changed anything at all.

We must accept that we are not perfect, not now, not if things would have been different, not ever. We are humans with broken hearts, warts, scars, and all.

Maybe we just need to realize that we are of great value to God in spite of it all. For Christ can shine through us. Isn't that more than we ever thought possible?

> *"Better it is to be of an humble spirit with the lowly, than to divide the spoil with the proud."*
>
> *Proverbs 16:19*

"If I Could Have Been There"

If I could have stepped out of the boat
no fear would I have had of the stormy sea,
for I know I wouldn't have been afraid
as His hand reached out for me.

If I could have seen Him when He stooped
to write some words of wisdom in the sand,
my compassion would have brought tears
as I reached out for the woman's hand.

If I could have been there in the garden
waiting patiently for my Lord to pray,
I would have never fallen asleep,
I'd never let them take Him away.

If I could have been there in the crowd
when asked whom to crucify,
I would have said "the thief, Barrabas,
please, don't let my Lord die."

And if I could have been there to carry
His cross on the way to Calvary,
the bloody brow of my Savior I would wipe
as He walked the road in agony.

But this all sounds too convenient, too proud
to think "what might have been,"
when I know I'm such a wretch of a soul
many times full of trouble and sin.

So, in reality I pray for strength because
I don't always withstand the storms of life,
and I need more compassion for others
and to share their burdens of strife.

Now asking, "Father, forgive my weakness"
when on my knees in the garden I pray,
for so often I fail to stand up tall enough
when weariness overtakes my day.

If you please, Father be by my side,
with "less of self" I humbly endeavor to be,
a vessel for your Son to shine through my life
and for others to see more of "Him" in me.

Amen

Just a Little -

I have a problem: I am compulsive, compassionate, a work-alcoholic. I can't do "just a little."

When I try my best to understand the character of God I find that the words "everlasting," "forever and ever" keep appearing. Doesn't sound like God does anything "just a little." Especially His love, His sacrifice.

In return God deserves more than to only give a part of ourselves, in service, in praise, in worship.

"So then because thou art lukewarm, and neither cold nor hot, I will spew thee out of my mouth."

Revelation 3:16

Just A Little

I bowed my knees to pray "just a little"
so my name would be still known,
just in case He forgot about me
I wanted Him to know I wasn't gone.

I remembered to say thanks "just a little"
when our table was filled with guests,
but other times my prayers I'd forget
as I laid my head to rest.

I would go to worship "just a little"
and sit quietly as I softly sang,
barely "just a little" so I could
say I praised His Holy name.

Then that night suddenly upon me
I heard these words of might…
**"remove him away from me,
cast him out of my sight.**

**For I gave him so much more,
even my only Son I gave
and in return 'just a little'
is all he gave in praise."**

Please Lord, I'll do more,
let me start over again
I will give my heart and my soul
if you let me once more begin.

Startled, I awoke from that dream
a night I don't want to relive,
then, I humbly bowed in prayer
with tears asking Him to forgive.

This could have been for real,
no second chance will there be,
I will ever more give my "all"
not "just a little" from me.

The Reading –

In our modern day of internet, email, satellite dish and cable we are bombarded with information. How much time do you allow God to communicate with you through His Word?

In earlier times I believe people desired God's Word more than they do today. They took the time to read, to study, to gain knowledge of God's commandments. Nothing we read or hear can be of more value than God's Word. Without it we are lost. Lost without direction. Lost without hope. Lost without faith. Lost.

"So then faith cometh by hearing, and hearing by the word of God."

Romans 10:17

The Reading

With great anticipation of all who were there,
we quietly sat on the floor or in an old easy chair.
Waiting for the grey haired man to settle down
he reached in his pocket and in that place he found
his spectacles all folded together & opening up those
placing them so slowly and gently upon his nose.

Blue sparkling eyes looked at each of us and then
he waited for a time to see if we had settled in
and at just the right moment a silence began
as the humble eyes were closed of this old man.
Not a whisper, nor a breath, or a sigh, not a word
until a soft tender "amen" from his lips was heard.

And as his wrinkled hand gently opened the "Book"
our eyes fixed upon the edges of gold that he took.
When the rustle of the pages stopped filling the air
knowing his fingers found the chosen place with care,
his voice sometimes trembled as he would read
yet we lingered for every word of truth and deed.

Not unlike a soft melody the words calmed our soul
about faithful men, and God's love written long ago,
but no matter where the old man's reading began
he ended the time always the same, again and again,
softly causing a tear down his cheek to be twirled
"lo, I am with you always, even to the end of the world."

The old man is gone now and not one took his place
sometimes I wonder if we are letting down our human race
by not following in the paths that are treasured and dear
by not reading to our young ones when they are near
by not honoring the elder and giving them a seat
and a time to read God's word as we sit at their feet.

"And I saw the dead, small and great, stand before God; and the books were opened: and another book was opened, which is the book of life: and the dead were judged out of those things which were written in the books, according to their works."

Revelation 20:12

Wisdom -

Getting out of a trap requires prayer, faith, and wisdom. The wisdom in understanding of where we are spiritually is vital to understanding of where we need to be and where to avoid.

> *"Whence then cometh wisdom? and where is the place of understanding?"*
>
> *Job 28:20*

> *"And unto man he said, Behold, the fear of the Lord, **that is wisdom;** and to depart from evil **is understanding.**"*
>
> *Job 28:28*

A Puller of Thorns

A Puller of Thorns – Why Was It You?

I always thought that if you were a Christian you automatically somehow have the gift of being able to help others physically, spiritually and emotionally in comfort, love and kindness.

I have found this not to be the case. It's not because God doesn't desire these characteristics that people don't posses them. I can find numerous passages that speak otherwise. Preachers give many sermons on helping our brother, uplifting and encouraging one another but the practice of doing so is far more difficult for most people than speaking the words.

The scriptures teach in Philippians chapter two, that we should look to the needs of others and esteem them before ourselves. Excuses and pride often keep us from doing so. But we can learn to do better. God doesn't command something we cannot do. On one hand I have found some that have such wonderful love of Jesus in their hearts that His light truly does shine in them. These are the ones that search and find a way to be a "puller of thorns." People that have struggles and trials know the pain of being trapped. We also know what eases that pain. We welcome "thorn pullers," you and I can be one too.

"But be ye doers of the word, and not hearers only, deceiving your own selves."
James 1:22

Why was it you?

Why did you hear more than most while I cried
when you saw my tears fall to the floor?
Why did you see deep inside my heart
when my pain overflowed even more?

Why didn't you say you didn't have time?
Why didn't you turn away?
Why did you comfort my soul
when you had more to do that day?

Why did you walk toward me;
why me, the one without?
Why did you pray for me?
Why did you believe and not doubt?

Why did you share my burden
when I had carried it for so long?
Why did you care about me,
when others didn't really hear my song?

When other people heard my cry
while they listened with one ear.
Why did you take one step more,
why did you even care?

For....

I believe that you believe
in what our Lord has said,
about bowels of mercy, compassion, & love
and all the verses in black and red

You really believe don't you,
In caring for a brother?
You believe that Jesus cares for me
and in loving one another.

You know you will see Him one day
because you love Him with all your heart,
With all your soul and with all your mind
and you're teaching me too that part.

Because you love me as yourself
and I believe you really do
And you try to live your life the best you can,
as He said in Matthew twenty two.

"Jesus said unto him, Thou shalt love the Lord thy God with all thy heart, and with all thy soul, and with all thy mind.
This is the first and great commandment.
And the second is like unto it, Thou shalt love thy neighbour as thyself."

Matthew 22:37 – 39

Let Me Share Your Burden –

People would tell me that helping others would take my mind off of my own problems. It does. But it doesn't take away all the pain and struggles instantly either. Some told me that when God said to "love thy neighbor as yourself," I couldn't truly love them until I love myself. I disagree. For I believe that in letting our love for others grow, even within our pain, we are increasing our love for ourselves at the same time. If we wait until we are "complete" if you will, we will never be of service to anyone but ourselves. If we shut out all others from the care God intends us to give, we rob them of our gifts and we shut ourselves out of the blessings that God will bestow upon them and us, which includes the joy and peace He promised.

> *"Now we who are strong ought to bear the weaknesses of those without strength and not just please ourselves. Each of us is to please his neighbor for his good, to his edification. For even Christ did not please Himself....."*
> *Romans 15: 1-3(NASB)*

Let Me Share Your Burden

When holes within a heart
begin to fill with hurt and dies,
because of some thing that within
begins to grow in size,
and become so overpowering
that love can no longer fit in,
someone else appears in the place
where you've always been.

So I will gladly carry my pain and sorrow
and I will take yours too,
and add yours to mine so you may be free,
if it takes the sorrows from you.
I will rid them from your heart
and remove your depths of despair
If you will be free and feel joy once more,
then this I will gladly bear.

Let it be me who feels the hurt inside
and let your heart begin to mend
from all the struggles and wounds
that grew from somewhere deep within,
so the joy will have a place to grow
so easy you won't even have to try,
I will pack the tears within my soul
so you won't have those tears to cry.

If you will share your burden with me,
for a length of time and more
so your eyes of hurt others see
will shine brightly again once more.
Let your smile once forgotten
again appear upon your face
I'll carry your load of hurt on my back
to see your tears erased.

Give God a joyful soul, accept His Grace
and let your heart shine,
showing your love and kindness and joy
again for all future time.
For no doubt, He will lift my burdens
and also the ones you let me share,
for I know he will let me carry
all that I am able to bear.

See, I think you have a duty
to fulfill your role God gave you in this life,
and you need a friend to share your burdens
when you have troubles and strife.
My part in life may be just this,
it may be to help you stay your arms today
just like Aaron and Hur helped Moses
as they were on their way.

When both our troubles are gone
and our earthly time on earth is thru
may we be together where the happiness,
joy and peace is true,
where no more sorrow, no pain,
no tears, no evil will there be,
praising the Lord for evermore
where beauty is all we see.

> *"Bear ye one another's burdens, and so fulfill the law of Christ."*
>
> *Galatians 6:2*

Fruits of a Christian Man –

Most people probably never think about the lasting impact another can have on our life, or the impact we may have on someone else's life. Then a disaster strikes. A death of someone we love or possibly a breakdown of our normal living patterns makes us think about every person in a path around us. We twirl around in our heads our impression of how they see us, view us. We question their actions and reactions. Sometimes we get it wrong. Other times we are very much in tune to their rejection or acceptance of us. How they treat us in respect to our failures and the acceptance of our successes is very much on our minds. Possibly this is why God told us that during trials we are made stronger.

Some broken souls take up a mask and hide themselves behind a pasted on smile and tell the world all is right and vow to never let pain in again. They rob themselves of others care and love. Some hold on to hope, overcoming, and now have become more ready to reach and touch others who have trials, burdens and heartaches. If we will allow the pain to be not in vain, we can desire to help others in need. We desire them to not suffer through alone. Just letting them know we care sometimes is all they and we need at the moment. The following selection contains examples of such emotions thanking people that reached and pulled a thorn from my flesh. Some are feeble attempts to lift them up to a higher ground.

I cannot do justice to these writings if I do not include private writings to people who have been in my life, willing to help. In doing so I hope you too will find those in your life and do not be discouraged by those who fail in their attempts. I truly believe God has placed some people just waiting for you. With prayer and seeking you will find them. God will not forsake you. He promised. My encouragement from these dear servants of Christ and brothers comes not only from the strengths they imparted that shined bright, but also from the weaknesses they did not vainly hide.

"For the grace of God that bringeth salvation hath appeared to all men,
Teaching us that, denying ungodliness and worldly lusts, we should live soberly, righteously, and godly, in this present world;
Looking for that blessed hope, and the glorious appearing of the great God and our Saviour Jesus Christ;
Who gave himself for us, that he might redeem us from all iniquity, and purify unto himself a peculiar people, zealous of good works."

Titus 2: 11-14

F r u i t s   o f   a   C h r i s t i a n   M a n

A man of reserve gentleness
sat with me today
he held my hand, shared my troubles,
and began to pray,

for himself asking nothing,
but from his soul to God's own ear
he prayed for me alone
but vain words I did not hear.

The air was still except
for the tear that dropped to the floor,
he silently asked God's comfort
upon me here once more.

The tender emotion swelling
in his eyes was so sincere
I felt wanting the best for me
was his reason to be near.

This wasn't the first and won't be the last
this friend will call
appearing from the shadows,
ready to catch me should I fall.

He softly talks about life's struggles
and about God's grace
with such wisdom and courage,
about rough times we all face.

You see, this man is different
from most people I know
for his Christianity is not put on display,
not just for show.

He keeps Christ deep within his heart,
a heart that's bound
with strings of love,
compassion and goodness all around.

Yet, he lowers himself to be a servant
to help all men
who need a kind word,
lifted up and a boost now and then.

My dear fellow-soldier in Christ
I know you don't understand
fully the strength you impart
when you hold out your hand.

I am not alone,
there are so many others that you feed
with your sharing of God's words
and your kind deed.

I think God must be smiling
down and so proud of you
because you show His Son
in all these things you do.

The Soul of Jonathan –

Rarely in this life someone comes along that you have spiritual connections with. I am not speaking about finding your "soul mate" nor am I speaking about "physical intimacy." Even though a spouse can be both, I am talking about someone that can with eyes pierce into what seems like your very soul. I am talking about a brother or sister that is bound together with you in Christ. This person cannot wear a masked smile in your presence, for it does no good for either of you, because it doesn't hide the pain, or tears within from each other.

The Soul of Jonathan Was Knit With the Soul of David

My soul heard you hurting
and I saw it in your eyes.
My heart felt the pain
you were holding inside.
For so many times
you were there for me,
showing me God's ways
and how things could be.

Caring and guiding
each step of the way,
you always gave more
than other men gave.
I cannot ever repay
your brotherly love to me
but I want you to know,
I'm always here if need be.

You know the words
much more than I and how they start,
"Be of good courage,
 and He shall strengthen your heart,"
for you know waiting for you
is your reward up above,
your robe, your crown,
the mansion, the love.

The gates will be open wide
for one of us, then the other,
until then while here on this earth
we will help one another.
You lift me up then
I'll hold out to you my hand,
while we make just one set
of prints in the sand.

Oh, Dear Brother –

How do you show Christ in your life? Do you know others are watching from a distance your character, your attitude without perhaps you even knowing? Oh sure, preachers, teachers, and leaders are analyzed and watched all the time. We even use their failures to excuse ourselves from worshiping God, calling them hypocrites, or to tell ourselves that if they don't have the right Christ like attitude then it's ok that I don't either. The thing about being in a desperate situation in life is that we tend to desire others in the church to be perfect, a protector, and a cure for all that ails us.

Let us examine our own lives. Do we live up to what God expects of us? God intended each of us to be an example for others, for each of us to show Christ in our lives. We are only going to answer for our own life. Only ours. Are we ready to give an answer for the portrayal of our life that others see?

> *"Pay close attention to yourself and to your teaching; persevere in these things, for as you do this you will ensure salvation both for yourself and for those who hear you."*
>
> *1 Timothy 4:16(NASB)*

Oh, Dear Brother

Oh, dear brother,
how I miss your wonderful smile,
and the twinkle in your eyes
has been gone for a while.
And how I miss that passion
your heart displayed,
for it would lift me up
every time I was dismayed.

For unknown to you,
your light shined so I could see.
Your grace, your kindness
and your sincere humility
would so often be an example
of how I may live,
your life gave me courage again,
that is what you give.

And, too, your voice in song,
sung with such depth,
truly admonished me, young man,
to take another step.
In helping me understand
the gifts we give each other,
you helped me so often
by showing your deeds, dear brother.

And so treasured soul,
please when you are discouraged,
know I pray God give you comfort
when you are so worried,
because you already gave
the comfort and the strength to me
by seeing Christ in your life,
showing what a life should be.

For you reminded me of me,
once when I was so young,
times when songs of praise
from my heart were sung.
So if you get a chance young man,
go high upon a hill,
and sing from your heart to Him
on High if you will.

Then you will feel His touch
and He will hear your heart,
and proclaim again His name
and with much thanks impart
such gratefulness by singing
glory to His name on High Adore,
then come and teach, and admonish
this old man once more.

> *"I will declare thy name unto my brethren, in the midst of the church will I sing praise unto thee."*
> *Hebrews 2:12*

God's Cowboy of Love -

Some people along my journey included very special people only one of which was a cowboy, a rodeo rider. (I call this his second choice.) His first choice in life is to be a compassionate, humble man of God's Word. A man who speaks God's Word with more love from his heart than any man I have ever met. Not only does he speak God's Word, he lives it. He is one of the people in my path who understands the struggles and trials of life and keeps getting up to ride again. Along his way his hand is always reaching out to give to another.

"And further, because the Preacher was wise, he still taught the people knowledge; yea, he pondered, and sought out, and set in order many proverbs.
The Preacher sought to find out acceptable words, and that which was written uprightly, even words of truth."

Ecclesiastes 12:9

Iron sharpeneth iron; so a man sharpeneth the countenance of his friend.
Proverbs 27:17

G o d ' s   C o w b o y   O f   L o v e

A Cowboy has the nerve
to enter the arena light
knowing a fury of power is against him,
ready for the fight.
Also aware of the dangers
always lingering there
sizing up the situation,
saddling himself down with care.

I know it hurts so bad
when one hits the ground
and hard to gain the strength
to go back for another round,
but the broncos waiting in line
need a man like you
one who has a few trophies
and also a few bruises or two.

A man that is girded with righteousness,
faith and fears,
who like David, slays giants one day
and another day sheds tears.
A man that can sit tall in the saddle
and overcome evil beasts,
yet not afraid to lower himself
to become "one of the least."

God has your trophy
awaiting along the gold street
and honoring and praising Him
you'll sit at His feet.
For I'm sure your name
is on the roster high up above,
and it wouldn't surprise me
if you are simply listed
"God's Cowboy of Love."

It's Easier -

I don't understand why we all cannot be full of the love that God intended us to have. I have and continue to mention this throughout this book. It is a great mystery to me. As Christian men and women, we know God's commandments to love our brother as ourselves, we know our obligation to the hungry, to the homeless. We hear and we teach that we should help those less fortunate than ourselves, and we should. I don't want to take away from the responsibility of supplying our neighbors their immediate physical needs. This help is our responsibility and is commanded in the Scriptures. We bless them with our kindness and will be blessed in doing so. Please, do not remove the obligation of helping others from the next statement.

In my search for brothers that are Christ centered and my quest to learn to help others I have found something profound in our service. Profound in the sense that when we do good works, we have the tendency to make a check mark by our name for that effort and mark it off our "to do" list. Profoundly greater is in the way we view our responsibility of helping our neighbor. How we are satisfied and how we pride ourselves on giving, while we ignore or even avoid the person themselves. We look upon them as a duty, a job, an item to be taken care of, but we fail to give warmth to their heart, hope to their soul, and meaning to their life. This is where we often stop and use the cliché "now it's up to you." Christ always taught "love" that includes more than a shirt or a meal.

There are many great and wonderful things we do, placing the cans of food in the donation box, helping in a shelter at Christmas, giving a donation to the family that lost their home. These good works are to be commended; they are as I said are commanded as well. I truly believe that we are God's servants and performing these duties brings joy into our lives. We should also warm the heart beneath the coat, give more love than money.

We should also strive to do the more difficult part of all, to lift them up. To give them hope that God is also watching over them without being condescending is most difficult.

We "the trapped" should also try to understand that sometimes it's difficult for those that remove a thorn in our lives to go beyond the physical. We as well can learn to be "thorn pullers" in its fullest sense. We must strive to acknowledge that after we remove the thorn, blood still flows. Don't forget the bandage of hope, love and compassion.

It's Easier

It's easier to give a hungry man a plate of food,
        or some dollars for a meal, and send him on his way
        than to mend his troubled soul upon a dreary day.

It's easier to love someone whom you've know for a little while,
        than to have charity to the spirit of the man
        who without someone's help can't even stand.

It's easier to quote a simple verse and be quick about your way,
        than to ask him to sit a while with you
        and wipe his tears when his story is thru.

It's easier to cover your ears, not get too involved in his troubles,
        than to let your kindness inside overflow
        and to help him up from the depths below.

It's easier to grab his hand when with trembling he reached out,
        than to be the first to say "are you all right?"
        when he may be too lonely or weak to ask tonight.

It's easier when they come to you, the tired, lost and sad,
        than to "walk toward them that are without,"
        but that's what we're told, that's what it's all about.

A Friends Helping Hand –

There are many who appear to be friends with smooth words and smiles that encourage us to be strong, acting ever so friendly. But if we fail or fall they quickly abandon the friendship. Then there are friends who are true, ones that do not shun us because of our failures. They are the friends that show us how to overcome trials by lifting us up with their helping hands. They reach out to impart strength, courage, and love, and just as Christ teaches they are truly "a brother's keeper" in watching over one another while we find our way. While recognizing their own burdens and faults they stick close by us, always there. It appears to me that they are trying to imitate God's love, for He never departs, never leaves us alone, always watching, always there, holding our hand.

> *"A man of too many friends come to ruin, but there is a friend who sticks closer than a brother."*
> *Proverbs 18:24*

> *"For I am the LORD your God, who upholds your right hand, who says to you, 'Do not fear, I will help you'."*
> *Isaiah 41:13*

A Friend's Helping Hand

Back some time ago you took hold of my hand
and you shed some tears with this old man.
Broken and torn was I and in need
of one to share my burden, hear my plea.

Without question, without fear, you felt my pain
when at that time you had so much of the same.
You put aside your cares for one you didn't know,
to comfort, to care and let your love show.

In all my many years I have never known
a man so caring, yet a man so strong,
who at times carry his own burden's around
and then adding another's as they are found.

Most have a limit to how much they give
but you, I cannot tell how deep your heart is,
for there's no bottom nor cap on your love
I feel for certain, you'll have a home up above.

For you can't fulfill the second command
to love your brother unless you stand
upon the first of his laws that He gave,
and the place of "first" for Him you save.

And once you saw me finally stand
you didn't even stop holding my hand.
You encourage, and strengthen me when weak
by the look in your eyes when His word you speak.

I try to be aware of things that I lack
for only a small step away, is the way back.
But, I know God holds my right hand yet again
and I also know my left is being held by a friend.

Me and My House

I Have Worth

When one brother told me, I have worth.
though it was hard for me to understand so,
another said I've been an example on earth
trying to follow the Lord, committed as I go.

As I feel they're so much more worthy than I,
they are much better in so many ways
I feel that they're righteous in God's eyes
not like my weakness in so many days.

But one told me, "I'm not greater than you,
for in God's sight, He respects all men,
and don't ever, ever believe that it's true;
for no man among us are above any sin.

All my brothers are yet no more or no less
than God's children following the command,
in loving their brother and doing their best
sharing my burden, holding my hand.

When once stood a shell of a man,
now I stand once more strong and tall,
while arrows still thrown now and again
fall short, don't pierce their target at all.

How do you convey the feeling inside
where pain held top position for so long,
where now love and contentment reside
and doubts and suspicions are gone?

Can you understand the feelings of a heart,
acknowledge the fact He's seen all your tears,
accepting God's love He had from the start,
taking away all your troubles and fears?

"Thank-You my Lord for having mercy on me
and guiding me and my brothers paths too.
The honor and glory we do give all to Thee!
Use me Lord, and let your love shine thru.

*"Are not two sparrows sold for a cent? And yet not one of
them will fall to the ground apart from your Father. But the
very hairs of your head are numbered. So do not fear; you are
more valuable than many sparrows".*

Matthew 10:29-31(NASB)

The Freeman Home —

Home? What makes it special? Some grow up in terrible circumstances and still call it home. Some have all the physical necessities, yet love is absent and it doesn't feel like a home at all.

It is your choice how your home is designed, how it is lived. Keep God the centerpiece upon your table. Keep thanksgiving upon your lips, His love in your heart, allow His mercy and kindness to influence your ways. Show obedience to Him in all you do.

Home is different for each of us, some are quiet, and some are loaded with activity. Children could be present or it could consist of aged grandparents shuffling around with minds active or forgetful. Still, home is home. A cardboard box, a shelter, an old Ford may be not so good of a home but hope can be there. We can allow God to be first in whatever circumstance we are in. Then one day home will be with Him.

*"And if it seem evil unto you to serve the LORD, choose you this day whom ye will serve; whether the gods which your fathers served that were on the other side of the flood, or the gods of the Amorites, in whose land ye dwell: **but as for me and my house, we will serve the LORD.**"*

Joshua 24:15

The Freeman Home

A light shines from your window
it brightens paths that's drear
and the light shining from your heart
tells everyone Christ is there.

The fruits of a Christian family
doesn't end with a son or daughter
your helping includes those in need
as commanded by our Father.

I know your home is a blessing to all
From it's door flows care and love,
and when God says it's time to rest
You'll trade this home for a home above.

Child of Mine –

We don't all get the chance to raise a child, hold them in our arms, or smell the beauty of a new born baby. But we all have been given the ability to love with that same sense of deep abiding unconditional love in our lives. For those of us who where blessed with children we know the times of simplicity and the times of complication in our relationships with them. We know all too well that one day, they must live their own lives. We hope, we pray that they will choose the right path. In addition to our limited abilities we know we won't always be there to take care of them, we ask our Father to do so in our absence.

What about us? Maybe we should not only think of rearing our child with the realization that God is present and loving, but maybe we should think of how our Heavenly Father would desire us to be.

Child of Mine

When just a child so close to me,
I would hold you against my chest,
feel your warmth and your heartbeat,
pat your back while you would rest.

Oh, how I loved you from the very start,
wondering who would you grow up to be.
I was so proud a father sitting there,
thinking, would you be like me?

So small and so tender, sweet smell of you,
my heart never felt such joy before,
I'll hold and take care of you,
I will cherish you for evermore.

Then as you grew into a youth,
the funny things you did, I'd laugh out loud!
Tell everyone the simplest tasks you accomplished,
being again so proud.

As time for school days came around
forcing a smile while I felt you leaving me,
subjecting you to this cruel world,
will you be frightened, how will you be?

If you need, call me and I'll come running,
If anyone hurt you.... then you would hear
"don't mess with my child," I will protect you,
I will always be near.

I tried, but couldn't keep all the pain
and all the hurtful heartaches from you,
like when you fell down, hurt your arm
or losing a friend because we moved away too.

Would you follow the things I taught you
as you grow older and learned your way?
I taught you about the ways of the Lord,
would you listen or be lead astray?

When you erred, it broke my heart,
it hurt because I wanted you to have the best,
but it could never separate me from my love for you,
your life, your soul, or happiness.

Now, I'm older and my love still strong for you,
I rejoice and cherish times we are together,
but at night when no one sees,
my pillow full of tears for you, thinking about forever.

Trying to be strong like when you were young,
sometimes I'm weak and what He said, I forget,
"Train up a child in the way he should go
and when he is old he will not depart from it."

And knowing the Lord heareth my cry
and he is near unto them who's heart is broken and torn,
I will trust in the Lord, asking Him to lead and protect you,
as I've always done, from the day you were born.

*"Now the days of David drew nigh that he should die; and
he charged Solomon his son, saying,
I go the way of all the earth: be thou strong therefore, and
shew thyself a man;
And keep the charge of the LORD thy God, to walk in his
ways, to keep his statutes, and his commandments, and his
judgments, and his testimonies, as it is written in the law of
Moses, that thou mayest prosper in all that thou doest, and
whithersoever thou turnest thyself:"*

1 Kings 2: 1-3

Daddy Can I Go? -

Rearing children is an awesome responsibility. We influence their lives, their character, morals, health and spirit. We guide our children through times with scrapped knees, bullies, lost kittens, lost friends, heartaches and successes. We always want the best for them don't we? We want them to succeed, to be healthy. Do we stop to think how we feed them spiritually on a daily basis?

"Children's children are the crown of old men; and the glory of children are their fathers."

Proverbs 17:6

"D a d d y ,   C a n   I   G o ? "

A grandchild age of four on Papaw's knees
asked "Going to church?," "Can I go please?"
Grandpa answered with a gleam in his eye
"Ask your dad if you can go today" was his reply
" For I would love it so much," Pawpaw say joyfully
and "I will be so proud that you sat with me."

Daddy said, "Not today," He didn't bring my clothes.
"Well, maybe next time you visit you will have those,"
answered the grandfather so tenderly and dear
just as a tear from his wrinkled face did appear.
The child asked "Next time, Daddy please can I go?"
"Don't bother Papaw you know he's getting old."

"Daddy? Tomorrow is Sunday once again,
Pawpaw will be waiting for me to go with him."
"Not Today, my child, I've got things to do
Maybe another time when our work is through."
Dad mumbles." "Besides, the drive is way across town,
and grandpa always goes, another time will be found".

"I know we should go" father explained once again,
"maybe next Sunday we'll both go together with him."
"Today Dad?" asked the child as he firmly stood.
"I know,... I said 'maybe', but today is not good.
I promise, some day, you'll see, we will all go together
just not today, you don't need out in such weather."

"You ready son?, it's almost time for services, young man."
the dad finally said holding tightly to his son's small hand.
Holding in the tears "He would have been so proud of you,
all dressed up so nice…. wait, let me tie your shoe."
"Son, I'm so sorry I .." ….., mumbling each sobbing word,
"Papaw's at church for the last time." was what the child heard.

"But whoso shall offend one of these little ones which believe in me, it were better for him that a millstone were hanged about his neck, and that he were drowned in the depth of the sea."
Matthew 18:6

Racing Toward The Finish Line –

Don't think you're not good enough to run the Christian race. If you do, you're wrong. You probably know all to well this world's view of success, the idea that we have to be first, that we must be the best. This somehow becomes our measurement of our worth. Sure, being good at something increases our confidence. A pat on the back for a job well done is often deserved and is uplifting. God gave us each special abilities, special love, special hearts to serve, none is better or worse than another. Your gift is different than mine. You are unique and are not to be measured by the gifts of others. God doesn't measure your life to mine, nor mine to yours. He only measures the heart of commitment to follow him. He takes note if we have chosen to enter the race or sit on the sideline.

"Wherefore seeing we also are compassed about with so great a cloud of witnesses, let us lay aside every weight, and the sin which doth so easily beset us, and let us run with patience the race that is set before us, "
Hebrews 12:1

R a c i n g   T o w a r d   t h e   F i n i s h   L i n e

I entered this race with joyful pride and wanting to win the prize,
I knew the task would not be easy, but I didn't realize
that the course set before me would test my every strength,
having to overcome hurdles, mountains, and hills at almost every
length.

Soon after the race got on it's way then I started to ask,
If I was even good enough to enter this long racing task.
I wandered off track a couple of times, just a little bit,
will that disqualify me at the finish line, will the Judge rule me
unfit?

The Judge, He wrote my name in a book when I entered this race,
I heard him say If I stay off the track, my name will be erased.
He is watching my every move, every time I slip and fall,
I'm trying hard to stay the course and be perfect once and for all.

I don't think I am qualified to finish a marathon in first place,
not even second or third I think, will I be in this race.
There are many runners in front of me, both women and men
that seem to have no trouble, I'll never get ahead and win.

How can I finish on top if perfection is not what He sees?
He may not let me finish, if near last is all I can be.
I know I read the rule about how we must be fit,
I committed it to memory, but I'm out of shape a bit.

As I approach the finish line some past trophies are displayed.
names such as Moses, Abraham, David, I see engraved.
One was given to Stephen, who when finishing died one day,
it is said his face appeared "angel like" when stones befell his way.

When the final ribbon was close in site, I glanced around to see
that not one woman, not one man was in front or behind me.
and as the Judge announced my name as I completed the race,
He said to me "well done, you finished, you *never* had to be in *first*
place."

A Great Leader –

Christ said "follow me". The apostle Paul said "imitate me as I imitate Christ". If someone was following us, was imitating our actions, would we be proud? Do we shy away from any appearance of being a leader in our work, home, school because we do not consider we have what it takes to do so? To often we look at what we are not good at rather than what we are capable of doing.

> *"For if there be first a willing mind, it is accepted according to that a man hath, and not according to that he hath not."*
>
> *1 Corinthians 8:12*

A Great Leader

Being a leader of the people we will probably never be,
such as Moses leading the chosen ones across the Red Sea.
No great giants will our hands ever slay,
with a few small stones and a sling one day

Nor will we be great commanders of men or be any bolder
than Joshua commanding twelve to load stones on their shoulders
to place as a sign for the children of man
that God is the Mighty, and Deliverer at hand.

Probably not wiser than Solomon will we ever be,
or build a temple to God, most beautiful to see.
No stripes will we bare of forty less one
like Paul and the apostles many times had done.

Remember as well when Moses looked around and saw no man,
he slew the Egyptian, and hid him in the sand.
And David was great in the days he was a king,
but he once angered God with a terrible thing.

No man has been perfect that was chosen of God,
to teach or lead his people that trod
upon this earth being encouraged to follow
the commandments of God, and the promises of tomorrow.

But we can be a leader through the trials of this life,
thru the pain and sorrow, troubles and strife.
Letting our light shine where ever we can,
helping others, guiding our fellow man.

Telling them that the peace of God shall keep their heart,
healing and mending right from the very start.
Preaching the gospel to all living creatures
telling them about Christ the Only One great teacher.

When We Are Old –

No getting around it, we will either die young or old. Too many times we waste our lives or feel like our lives wasted us. If our life wasn't interrupted or complete due to some tragic illness or accident then our time here on earth is spent mostly exactly how we decided it would be. We can't blame others or the government or even God.

God gave us the power to choose. We may not be rich, or powerful if we measure our life by this world's measuring stick. But if we have a peace from God in our hearts we will be rich, we will be viewed as a child of His, strong in His kingdom.

Sometimes we need to reflect and ask ourselves the hard questions. How have I lived my life? Will it be acceptable to God?

"And inasmuch as it is appointed for men to die once and after this comes judgment"

Hebrews 9:27 (NASB)

When We Are Old

When our hair is grey, our days seem almost gone
what do we think our destination will be?
When our youth has slipped away
what will our children see?

When our eyes get more dim each year
will our heart still be able to see?
And our ears being less in tune
will our life be bound or free?

If our bones hurt with pain
and our fingers bleed,
if our feet are swollen and tired,
will our soul be still in need?

If death is knocking on our door
will we be ready to go?
Or will we be asking for a little more time,
will we be begging so?

Have we committed to memory
the things that are the best?
Things true, honest, lovely and good,
thoughts that help pass the test.

Do we find the peace of God
well within our hearts?
Did we search the scriptures at all,
did we ever start?

Will we tell our children when
it is time to go, I cannot stay,
like David told his son before he died
"Keep the Lord thy God and walk in His ways."

Broken Heart –

It's rough going through our trials, fighting our own demons, struggling with temptations of this world to get on solid ground. All seems worse when we lose someone we love, we feel burden upon burden, sorrow upon sorrow. I still have difficulty in telling you that are grieving what you need to hear, or what I should say. I have found that this poem *"Broken Heart"* has said some things I could not speak with my lips.

Broken Heart

No one can ever imagine,
the pain within a heart
when the loss of someone
so dear, tears your heart apart.

As kind words of "I'm so sorry
for your loss" are spoken,
you nod and say "thank-you"
but it doesn't mend a heart that's broken.

You wanted this not to happen,
not today, not at all.
And bearing your sorrow all within
while tears begin to fall.

So, comfort is hard to find,
when a love leaves this earth.
No one but you will understand
the treasure they were worth.

So, I can't tell you exactly
what you may need to hear,
but these two special verses
keep ringing in my ear.

"The righteous cry,
and the Lord heareth," the verse starts,
and tells us He is near to them
that are of a broken heart.

Psalm 34:17-18

Staying Free

Staying Free -

If you have read this far then maybe you have found something of value to you and that means that I have accomplished my goal. I am not going to use the cliché "hang in there" or "when you're at the end of the rope, tie a knot in it and hang on." I disliked hearing these. You probably do too, when all you want to do is to "let go of the rope."

The thing you must do is to "let go of the pain." Realize that you have been given a way out of the brambles and all you have to do is search, knock, and seek and you will find it. Fully, and I mean absolutely, completely with all your heart TRUST in God. PRAY for wisdom, guidance and forgiveness. READ His Word. Understand you will never be perfect and accept that simple fact, and at the same time watch for confirmation of your worth. God doesn't create anything of no value. That includes you and me.

This last section hopefully will give you hope, courage and something other than yourself and your struggles to hold on to. Hopefully it will give you ways to find the courage, joy, beauty and strength that God alone promises to you. I have had many say "I can't do it for you," "you have to do it yourself." Partially true. They can't, I can't do it for you, but you don't have to do it by yourself, either. That's one thing of which I am certain. You may even look around and see no one by your side, and you say "Look, do you see anyone here?" "I am alone!" NO, you are not. That is when you need to get down on your knees and thank Him for being with you, being right by your side. God said "I" "I, the Alpha, the Omega" "I, the Lord, God Almighty" "I WILL NOT forsake you." Thank Him for His promise. Thank Him for keeping it. Then look up and ask Him – please use me today to help another.

He may choose to answer your prayer differently than you expect. He may be working in ways you don't understand that are the best at the moment. But He will not forsake you if you don't turn away. It is your choice to be separated from Him. Not His.

> *"Make sure that your character is free from the love of money, being content with what you have; for He Himself has said, "I WILL NEVER DESERT YOU, NOR WILL I EVER FORSAKE YOU," so that we confidently say, "THE LORD IS MY HELPER, I WILL NOT BE AFRAID, WHAT WILL MAN DO TO ME?"*
> *Hebrews 13: 5-6 (NASB)*

My Prayer For The New Year –

When you realize that no matter what others think of you in this life, it doesn't have to hinder your ability to be at peace. The problem with ourselves to often is that we become just like the very ones that we condemn. We want to withdraw from the so called "good" people that don't understand. We want to become bitter toward those who do not show care. The road goes both ways my friend, learning to love and care for those who think they are above us is our responsibility and command. Love is not like a river, love flows both directions. Have you ever helped a stranger that you knew was "better off" than you and without any expectation of any thing in return? When you can do that with joy in your heart, you are well on your way to a peace that passes all understanding. Do good to all men.

The one thing we must do now is to decide to allow our past to hinder us or to look forward to the future. When all we focus on is the doom and gloom of the future or the failures and pain of the past, the future doesn't look like a good place to be. So let today be your "new year" a "new beginning" being thankful for all the blessings you have.

> *".... but one thing I do; forgetting what lies behind and reaching forward to what lies ahead, I press on toward the goal for the prize of the upward call of God in Christ Jesus."*
>
> *Philipians 3: 13-14 9 (NASB)*

M y   P r a y e r   F o r   T h e   N e w   Y e a r

As the old year passes on I pause just to say
Thank-You dear Lord as the new one is about to begin,
for the blessings I received this last year
don't stop just because of the calendar's end.

Others may have seen my meager home
or my weak frame and said "isn't it a shame,"
But, I thank-you for my blessings and my promise
for a home up above, from whence my Savior came.

A few passed me by when I fell down and failed,
though they knew how hard I had tried;
but you, Dear Lord, You held my hand each day
and You are always by my side.

Many may have noticed the tattered edges
of my clothes I tried to hide from public display
but these are only temporary I know,
for my robe so white is waiting for me someday.

Others may have thought that some were out
of the reach of Your loving arms and attention,
But I know you hear my prayers for them, Father,
for Your mercy reaches beyond our comprehension.

Some saw my tears flow because of loss, or trials,
and thought I may had lost touch with reality,
but I know my heart is consoled by your love,
and your forgiveness of my sins always comforts me.

Others may think I don't have enough,
or some think I have much more than needed,
but I know I'm just passing thru and my reward is above,
where You and your Son are seated.

While singing and praising you some may still think
that it is only a superficial tradition,
But my worship describes the love of why Christ died
in offering me the gift of salvation.

So, I'm not asking for an easier new year,
for the year has made me stronger as I received your loving touch,
my prayer for the new year again is let me love you
this year, only let it be twice as much.

"And I will make them and the places round about my hill a blessing; and I will cause the shower to come down in its season; there shall be showers of blessing."

Ezekiel 34:26

Now I Understand

When I am sad or discourage, and feeling all alone,
I don't worry about my troubles for they will soon be gone.
For He will stand beside me helping carry my load
and He not forsake me because I am of His fold.

I know He stands beside me
holding my hand.
He will not forsake me,
He will understand.

When others about me are tempting me to stray,
I won't give in to their pleas nor give into their way.
I ask God to hold me in the shadow of His wing
and He will guide and protect me always from everything.

I know He stands beside me,
holding my hand.
He will not forsake me,
He will understand.

When I have feelings no one understands,
I take them to the Father above, lift up my hands,
asking Him to be with me through each and every day
and He will give me peace as I go along my way.

I know He stands beside me,
holding my hand.
He will not forsake me,
He will understand.

When my time on earth is over, may I then see,
that every scar and every tear was turned into a purpose to be.
Every battle was worth the fight, every pain a joy,
I fought the fight and will live with Him now forevermore.

He knows I stood beside Him
holding His hand,
I did not forsake Him
Now I understand.

*"For now we see through a glass, darkly; but then face to
face: now I know in part; but then shall I know even as also
I am known. "*
1 Corinthians 13:12

Armor Fitting –

I think one of the most important lessons I have learned is that God isn't going to change His scheme of things, change His plans, or slack up on His commandments just for me. He won't change my purpose just because I have had my share of difficulties in life. He isn't going to change it for you either. We must realize that God in His infinite wisdom has placed a method of salvation and of service to Him that was designed by His wisdom, not ours.

God's wisdom, which is so much higher than ours has determined and put into place the ultimate battle gear to fight the devil, the evil, the false teachings, the sins of this world. We must put on His armor. We can only succeed if we accept His will, His service, and His plan. Maybe you have tried to wear His armor before and it didn't fit you. Don't try to have the armor tailored to fit you. You will weaken it. You are not qualified, nor am I to make any changes. You must, I must grow to fit the armor He designed.

> *"Suffer hardship with me, as a good soldier of Christ Jesus. No soldier on service entangleth himself in the affairs of this life; that he may please him who enrolled him as a soldier.*
> *2 Timothy 2:3-4*

Armor Fitting

With much pride
I entered the army of the King,
my suit is prepared for battle,
my armor shining.

As I entered the gate,
there it was, made for me.
So grand, so majestic,
mighty warrior would I be.

Trying to bind my garments,
"this belt is way too big"
"you've made a mistake" said I,
"I can't wear this rig!"

"See, the shield is too heavy,
the helmet oversized,
if I have to wear this,
then don't be surprised

when I fall down in battle,
for you didn't listen to me
I can't wear this heavy thing,
why can't you see?"

"If I would send you to war
with the armor that you dream
the powers of darkness
would tear each and every seam.

I know what you need,"
said He *"to keep you safe with Me,*
I go before you into battle,
I see things before you see."

"Yes, the shield is large
because faith can conquer all,
strengthen yourself warrior,
shod your feet to stand tall.

Grow into your breastplate,
do not have any evil ways,
the helmet I gave will save you,
it will bring you home someday.

The sword is two-edged
to carry by your side
when you put the whole armor on,
you'll be ready for the ride.

See, it's not the armor
that's too large, or too heavy of a load,
it's the soldier that's got to grow,
he has to fit the mold.

Now when you finish the fight,
when the battle you have won,
I will no longer call you my soldier,
I will call you.... My son."

Wherefore take up the whole armor of God, that ye may be
able to withstand in the evil day, and, having done all, to stand.
Stand therefore, having girded your loins with truth, and
having put on the breastplate of righteousness, and having
shod your feet with the preparation of the gospel of peace;
withal taking up the shield of faith, wherewith ye shall be able
to quench all the fiery darts of the evil one.

And take the helmet of salvation, and the sword of the Spirit,
which is the word of God:

Ephesians: 6: 13-17

Dream or Vision –

Now comes the beginning of your new life if you choose to take it. For I firmly believe that if you do not have a vision for your future you will perish. Your body may continue to exist for a time, but you, you inside will perish along with your soul if you cannot envision God's work for you. If you cannot see His love, His grace, mercy, compassion, forgiveness and allow all these and more to give you a vision to do something tangible in you life, then my friend, you are in danger. Understand this, the last part of this verse is not some "magic potion" it is REAL, it is TRUE, and it is a FACT. "He that keepeth the law, happy is he." Happy will you be when you keep God's commands. Treasure His love. Be in His service. Obey Him, Praise Him, Worship Him. Happy you will be.

"Where there is no vision, the people perish: but he that keepeth the law, happy is he."

Proverbs 29:18 (KVJ)

Dream or Vision

Father, I had this dream
of how I know I'm to be.
Giving myself in service,
giving my all to Thee.

I now realize, O Lord
the dream has not come true.
It was only in my mind
It wasn't a vision that I would do.

For a vision Father, has power
a dream has none at all.
With a vision I will not perish,
but a dream will let me fall.

A dream only uses imagination
and it only gives me a start,
but a vision will use my hands
as it grows within my heart.

As I begin to understand just a little
about your love and things to be,
ever since time began YOUR vision
was how to save someone like me.

Still, you gave me a choice
to sit and dream my life away,
or rise in obedience to you,
making YOUR vision mine, today.

The Final Letter –

As far as I know no one has been able to write a letter from the grave. But I wonder if I could do so what would I say? Would words of love, wisdom, concern come to the forefront of my mind? All I know about death is that it is described as: one, the separation of this body and spirit, and two, there is a difference in those who die "in Christ" and those who die "outside of Christ," with the latter being an ultimate death of separating us from God. I don't mind the separation of this worn, tired body from the spirit. The second separation, I don't even want to entertain. We read in Galatians 3:27 "For as many of you as have been baptized into Christ have put on Christ." I want Christ in my life. I want others to see Christ in my life. I want to be with Him in eternity. Don't you?

Here on this earth we consume our lives with numerous things, mainly – living and all that entails. Either our life was good or our life was not-so-good. The joys, the sorrows, the trials, the successes of our lives will be in time forgotten by those left behind. Even our being trapped in the brambles, too will be whispered for only a short time. A generation or so, possibly less, our lives are only thought of by the fading memories of something in our friends and families past. That's just the way it is. Few of us will be or have ancestors of great historical significance but hopefully more of us have had mothers, fathers, grandmothers or grandfathers, or that special uncle, aunt or friend, brother or sister that had a special "life." I am not speaking of being special in worldly possessions, goods or career successes. I mean special in the sense that Christ shined through their life, they made a difference! I have written about those "special" people. I have written to you and about you.

If your letter is not what you would want it to be, change your life. You can stay trapped in the brambles, bleeding, hurt, and crying. Or you can say, see this scar? This is when I struggled. See my joy? This is being "free". You have all of God's grace and mercy to rely upon to be free and live a life that is full of joy, contentment, and love for the rest of your days on this earth.

So? What would you say to your friends, family if you could write one last letter from beyond the grave? Wherever you are after death would most assuredly influence what you would say. Too late for any changes and the facts only are allowed.

Don't get comfortable with the pain. Don't allow your own blood to stain you permanently. Don't stay trapped. If you first will start reading God's Word, asking in prayer for His help then He will hear. Seek. You will find. Call on Him. He will answer. Ask for relief. He will heal. Ask for forgiveness. He will forget your past. Ask to serve and He will find you work. Then you will be freed and I truly hope my friend you can say. I'm "freed from the brambles." If you could write one final letter after you die, what would it say?

I truly hope you can say you have been "freed from the brambles" by the help of a friend.

"And the LORD spake unto Moses face to face, as a man speaketh unto his friend ...."

Exodus 33:11

The Final Letter

Dear Family & Friends,

I've just moved away, I'm not really gone
but don't you worry; it's time to be strong,
for have no fear, that I've gone away
I didn't have control as "to go" or "to stay".

But now that I'm here, I hope you'll understand,
I don't want to come back from this new land.
And let me try to tell you why if I may,
about this place and why I like this way.

The city has no crime, no murder, none who steal.
It's amazing how everyone lives, how they feel.
I haven't seen one tear, no cries are heard,
no war or bad news, not even a harsh word.

And all who dwell here are treated the same.
There's no rich, no poor, no sick, no lame.
Everyone has this "glow of happiness",
and nowhere is found anything less.

No place have you ever seen comes near,
to the beauty and glory that is seen here.
Children and old together gather around,
"together" in mind and spirit are they bound.

Praising and singing is a wonderful pleasure,
and my heart's "full" way beyond measure.
And I have even seen a real angel up close,
we joined in together praising our glorious Host.

And I have seen our God, He even knew my name.

By His side, His Son sat on the throne they claim.
I was given a spotless white robe and a shining
crown,
as I humbly before our Holy Father bowed down.

I can't exactly explain the sights from here,
no earthly words can ever come near.
So you will just have to come and see me,
and let me show you around this amazing city.

I left a map for you to my new home by my bed.
It tells you the way and His words are in red.
Read it with care and follow them at all cost,
follow only His path so you won't get lost.

And then when our God calls you home,
You will know I'll be here, you won't be alone
and you & I can walk the streets joyfully,
We can praise His name for all thru eternity.

Remember God is not only up here,
He's always with you, He is always near.
So take care my friends, my family,
see you later when your are here with me!

With all my Love,
Danny

The Beginning

Now, you can be free. It's time for you to write your vision……...

I'll start –

Trust in Him today……………….. In Everything